The BETTER HALF

The BETTER HALF

Featuring
HARRIET
&
STANLEY
PARKER

ace books
A Division of Charter Communications Inc.
A GROSSET & DUNLAP COMPANY
51 Madison Avenue
New York, New York 10010

THE BETTER HALF

The Best Laughs of THE BETTER HALF, Volume I
Copyright © 1981 The Register and Tribune Syndicate, Inc.
All Rights Reserved
ISBN: 0-441-05497-8
First Ace Printing: December 1981
Published simultaneously in Canada
Printed in the United States of America

"Remember when I used to spend $20 and had to ask you to help me carry in the groceries?"

"No, Stanley didn't score a hole-in-one with it. It's the only golf ball with which he ever played an entire round without losing it."

"She needs either a better voice or a lower-cut gown!"

"Anyone who wants to help in the yard, snore."

"I wonder how come there are so many more people
on earth in mid-December than the rest
of the year?"

"Sorry, I just gave at the office."

"What do you mean, 'Merry Christmas'? Would you care to step outside and say that?"

"Being the Christmas season and all, I figured you'd want me to keep the ten spot I found in your pocket lining."

"Stanley just had his stomach pumped out. I forgot
to tell him that I emptied that flask he carries
in the glove compartment and filled it
with gasoline for emergencies."

"The bus will probably be late, so why don't you
build a snowman for the children waiting
on the corner?"

"Do you have one that's a summer coat on one side and a winter coat on the other?"

"The eternal triangle — you, me, and the alarm clock."

"It's stopping — you're starting!"

"Do you think we should wish the Allens a Merry Christmas after what our dog did to their garden?"

"All I want for Christmas is a 'paid in full' stamp on our bills from LAST Christmas."

"Look, a lady Santa. I wonder if she'd like to sit on MY knee and hear what I want for Christmas?"

"I gave Stanley the camphorated oil compress as you suggested, Doctor, but he spit it up!"

"Trees are pretty stupid. When it starts to get cold, they undress!"

"I've got the answer, to all of our problems! We'll throw out the stereo and TV, put a 1947 calendar on the wall, and lock the doors permanently!"

"Want to go on a cruise? I think we've got some logs we can lash together."

"I believe Stanley thinks of this place as 'Harriet's Bar and Grill.'"

"Take those back where you found them and bring his
work gloves."

"I know they're expensive, but my feet are tired of traveling economy class."

"If I buy $10 worth of dog scraps, would you throw in a small steak for me and my wife?"

"He keeps his weight down all right — it's all below his chest."

"Do you have to tell anyone that I dropped a dumbbell on it?"

"Would you care to hear a humdrum excuse about why I'm late — or an exciting, adventure-packed account of a pat royal flush?"

"Good news! You'll soon be going along with the current trend of putting your money into gold."

"Stanley watched too many sports events on television. This morning when I told him 'It's twenty to seven,' he just rolled over and asked, 'Who's ahead?'"

"Are you sure this isn't an antique mirror you bought for me? It has a lot more wrinkles than my old one."

"I see you're having as much trouble making ends meet there as you are financially."

"I first took this as a summer job while working for my doctorate, and then got married and couldn't afford to quit."

"That shows how our outlooks on life differ. You see
my paunch as evidence of my gluttony, but I see it
as a glorious symbol of your culinary expertise."

"I'd sure like another great breakfast like yesterday
morning — but I just don't have the time
to stop at Bert's Beanery."

"I wanted to buy you a gold watch but I couldn't get
the claw in the penny arcade to drop right."

"Now is the time for all good men to come to."

"Until he mentions prices, this place has all the nostalgia of the old-fashioned butcher shop."

"He's a self-made man — but then he never was very handy."

"There's a special on today. Buy one shoe for $35 and you get the other shoe free!"

"Of course, the historical accuracy of my story has been sacrificed in the interest of the main character's security."

"Perhaps the thing you don't like about it is the drip in the bucket seat."

"Modern airmail is certainly fast . . . this letter from Hawaii is still a little warm!"

"If seedless grapes are possible, why hasn't anybody developed a boneless chicken?"

"Can't you just fish the shoe out and seal it up again?"

"Somewhere along life's way, there was a malfunction of his ambition."

"I wish you'd phone when you'll be home late so I won't worry. By the way, I came across a clause in your insurance policy I didn't understand."

"It was bad enough somebody else wore the exact same pantsuit — what made it worse was it looked better on HIM!"

"She probably had her hands out for money all the time."

"I set the alarm for a half hour earlier tomorrow
'cause I'll have to get shopping money from you."

"You'll have to put this size 4 on yourself. I never
could stand the sight of blood."

"Sure, I know our motto, but I'll still wait."

"I think I'll lower our standard of living and go back to bed!"

"I know I SHOULDN'T HAVE, but I formed a mental picture of what life was going to be like if I WOULDN'T HAVE."

"Next November me and the boys are planning a trip to the North Pole to try to shoot a few polar bears and old you-know-who."

"May I interrupt this telecast to wish you a Happy New Year?"

"I just made out my New Year's resolutions . . . no more staying home alone while you bowl . . . no more cigar ashes on the carpet . . . no limit on my shopping"

"Before we enter, let's observe a moment of silence for our husbands' next three paychecks."

"We're having a two-for-one sale today — how about the second one for Mr. Husky?"

"I never wasted time on games in my youth. At age 10, I zeroed in on laziness and by age 20 I held the national crown."

"I wish they'd invent a diet food that was MINUS a few hundred calories so you could eat something decent with it."

"These chocolates are ruining my diet. I had to eat about a pound of soft ones, which I hate, before I came across one chewy one!"

"Miss Zinn's lawn is always greener than ours. Guess I'll just mosey over and ask her how she does it."

"Besides the regular sales tax, will he have to pay an amusement tax?"

"Do you have something to drive my husband insanely jealous?"

"If you ask me, you never really lost any weight —
you just misplaced it."

"I see there's going to be a new two-dollar bill is-
sued. Actually, we have it now — it's
called a five."

"As a consumer, I sometimes feel I'M being consumed."

" . . . . That moves you another two inches down my shopping list . . . . keep it coming."

"And you haven't even been in it yet! The trees are
obviously trying to commit suicide just at
the thought of it."

"We have binoculars for different purposes. First of
all, are you a hunter, a bird watcher, or
a peeping tom?"

"Why don't you put a lock under your pillow —
maybe there's a toupee fairy."

"Certainly you're not over the hill. Why, you've never
even started up the incline!"

"I hope Harriet saw that big fur sale ad in today's paper. If she did there'll be a good supper waiting for me."

"Has a sexy blonde I saw in the neighborhood selling magazines been here yet?"

"I would have thrown him out long ago if I didn't have
so many dresses with zippers in the back."

"I got a traffic ticket for running through a red light
— pole and all."

"Is it my fault that you're such a lousy teacher?"

"We're getting there. Our cup doesn't actually run over, but I think a drop just trickled down the side."

"I hid your credit cards where you'll never find them
— in your darning basket."

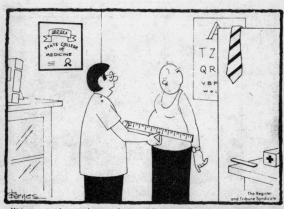

"You ought to lose about 30 pounds. A word to the
wide is sufficient."

"I'm not cynical about politicians. I believe everything the Democrats say about the Republicans, and everything the Republicans say about the Democrats!"

"I'm not sure, but I think it's a program about our plumber."

"Instead of shorter work hours I wish the unions
would work toward legislating a few extra
hours between midnight and 7:00 A.M."

"Stanley, why don't you stop by after work and have
too many with the boys?"

"No thanks, I already have an automatic dishwasher
complete with baby blue eyes and a cute,
pudgy figure."

"No, they're not too heavy for me, ma'am. It's a lot
harder when I help the manager carry the cash
receipts to the bank!"

"When Harriet's mother had her face lifted it broke the crane."

"Maybe you'll relax about the new car now that we're past that 'first scratch'."

"I wish they'd get fat enough to want to have their jaws wired shut."

"That's just a hobby of hers. Harriet's real interest is cleaning ovens."

"What happened to the Giants and the Braves?"

"Don't sit on the chair, I just painted it."

"Pick your fingers up off the floor and come with me.
It's time for lunch."

"Mr. Parker is doing fine. He should be up and around in another $30."

"I think you ought to put up some new seed packets.
These are getting pretty faded."

"I can't finish this steak, Bert. Give me a wifey bag."

"If I were to describe progress on your new diet in golf terminology, I would say that you double bogeyed the first hole!"

"Now, which side is up?"

"I call my wife 'Blue Monday', because I hate to face her too!"

"Lucky you didn't get a ticket! Your meter's expired!"

"It so happens that those two items on my charge account, 'A Passionate Embrace' and 'Blackmail', are merely perfumes!"

"I remember now . . . we decided last fall we couldn't afford both a distemper shot for the dog and a flu shot for you."

"This boat has such a broad beam, I think I'll name it after your mother."

"It's just another of those crank letters from the Internal Revenue Service."

"Let me know if you're baseball fans and I'll make a special effort to have it fixed in time for the World Series."

"Sorry . . . I just gave."

"On the last photo, Stanley would like an enlargement
with the fish triple size, and the rest of the scene
double, and his stomach left the same."

"Spring is finally here. The daffodils are blooming and
the lawn mower is waking from its long winter nap!"

"You have a choice for dinner tonight. Small . . . medium . . . or a large can?"

"One thing sure . . . anyone who snatches your purse won't be able to run with it."

"Mind if I make it a duet?"

"Cheer up! Remember, April showers bring May double-headers."

"I wonder if this stuff is printed green or if it gets that way staying in your wallet so long?"

"Let me have a young chicken that let her figure go to pot."

"This is it, Rogers! I just saw the price of Christmas cards and I've decided we can't afford friends anymore."

"Mind if I watch when you install the periscope?"

"Inflation? That's like falling in love. You don't know
what causes it and there's nothing
you can do about it."

"You may be interested to know that harmless little
snowfall the weatherman told us to expect has just
cut us off from civilization."

"We're actually leaving early! Are you sure that you
didn't leave out any ingredients?"

"The sale starts in 15 minutes — could you cut short
the counseling and let go of the
other end of the twenty?"

"I WOULD start the day with a song, but I can't think of one sad enough."

"I wish you wouldn't buy aspirin tablets in bottles with child-proof caps!"

"Forget about a silly present — go over to Schultz's Butcher Shop and get him a standing rib roast."

"If I loan the flour and egg, will you loan me a piece of the cake?"

"He tried doing cartwheels when I kiddingly told him
I was going home to Mother."

"Before I give you the bill, I suggest you fasten your
seat belt first."

"Cagey, isn't it, the way they place aspirin commercials in these nerve-shattering newscasts?"

"We men owe a debt of gratitude to the inventor of high heels — without them women would NEVER stop shopping!"

"You'll probably like this picture . . . it flatters your gall bladder."

"Haven't you got anything better to do than meet me here every morning at 6:30?"

"This is what I like — the head with the built-in coffee break!"

"We had a little flurry of excitement last week. Stanley went berserk and lifted a heavy box for me."

"Arise, sire. Once again the rosy-fingered dawn touches her magic wand. The snow on the rooftops and the world of commerce eagerly await thy coming."

"You expected long-stemmed WHAT?"

"I get the impression the English language is changing so fast they may recall my dictionary."

"Only four bills so far this month . . . have you been sick?"

"If you're trying to cover it all up, there's still some parts showing through."

"The house is in the middle of a snow trap. See what you can do with this club."

"That tenderloin you sold me didn't live up to its first two syllables."

"Come on, Stanley — I can fit you in while George is hanging up his coat."

"It's partly my fault . . . I didn't hide my husband's tools as well as I thought."

"He remembered to remove the top of his pajamas before taking his shower . . . not bad for a Monday morning."

"I held my breath, took out my upper bridge, lifted one leg, and I still haven't lost an ounce on this new diet!"

"I'm glad you wanted to see it on TV. I would have hated to hear you grumble about tossing four bucks down the drain."

"This is one time I wish we had a 6-year-old here — so he could open the safety cap on these aspirins for me."

"I SHOULD get a new one. My old one's worn out at the knees."

"I left the car at the garage. The way I understand it,
the automatic transmission got into a fight
with the automatic clutch."

"Prime interest rates are coming down . . . why
aren't your prime beef rates?"

"Stanley's decided to go out for the 10-yard waddle this season."

"I'd like to have it washed and ironed."

"Well, I call it an obscene call from the phone company — when they call you to pay the bill!"

"Stanley won't buy me a fur coat because it would ruin the hide of an irreplaceable animal — his pigskin wallet!"

"This isn't much of a trade — one double martini for one week's pay!"

"I can remember when the same money bought the groceries, paid for my hair-do, and added a little bit to my secret absconding fund."

"Harriet's an enigma. She has a shelf full of cook-books and a freezer full of frozen dinners."

"I slashed expenses last month — everything was charged on one credit card so that it will take only one postage stamp to pay our bills."

"I'm just now getting indigestion from last Thursday's
$12.45 roast!"

"Better stay out of sight while I'm using this vacuum
— the temptation might be too great."

"Obviously, my mother-in-jaw."

"And I say that without fear of contradiction. I say ANYTHING without fear of contradiction! Harriet is away visiting her mother this week."

"I said take out the GARBAGE!"

"Your mother was in a pretty good mood tonight.
Your dad only had to take his ulcer medicine twice."

"See if they can do anything about that tendency of people to take me for your son."

"I think I know the trouble — this little piggie that's been eating roast beef is not so little anymore."

"And now the Oscar for bringing home the bacon
. . . the envelope, please."

"Stanley, what did you say to my geranium?"

"The only thing the burglar took was our new burglar-proof lock which cost $75."

"We'll have to eat out. I just washed the kitchen floor and can't do a thing with it."

"Gift wrap it. I want to surprise my wife on her birth-day."

"I can't get it into Harriet's head that low-low payments plus low-low payments plus low-low payments equals high-high payments."

"It had to happen sooner or later, but it's still a blow
— I was called 'old timer' at the office today."

"Guess what! Officer Clancy told me I'm the best per-
son in the city at filling out accident reports."

"Do you have a steak with a price that doesn't ruin the flavor?"

"With the price of meat the way it is, I assume that's
not really a roast but a piece of burned wood,
and this is all a bad dream!"

"For your information, for the remainder of the winter we are not accepting postcards from any-where that palm trees grow."

"My husband asked you for a rough estimate, but he didn't mean THAT rough!"

"Since I'm stuck with you for life, I wish you'd try to show a little."

"You're a bill collector? What a coincidence. We're the biggest bill collectors in the block!"

"Harriet won't say who gave her this recipe — she tries to say nothing but good about her mother."

"For heaven's sake, let's not get into an argument now! It's too hot to close all the windows."

"Your weeds are in my flowers again."

"We buy our dirt direct, and pass along the savings to our customers."

"I have an idea! Where's that teddy bear you won at
the shooting gallery?"

"Bills, bills, bills! I'll remember this when it comes time
for your Christmas tip."

"Would you drive a while, dear? I need to cure my hiccups."

"We're taking a second honeymoon. My wife went to the mountains."

"I'm here for the very same reason you're
here — MONEY!"

"Well, you see, down is up."

"Good afternoon, sir. I wonder if your wife might be interested in our Jiffy Craft Electric Lathe?"

"Rescue squad? This is Bert, again. Two more of them just ordered the 'soup supreme.'"

"Hark! I think I heard a price drop!"

"THAT'S the middleman that our high grocery prices are going to!"

"Hold it! This calculator only goes to six figures!"

"What do you recommend for a household pest that weighs about 180 pounds?"

"I'll need only $3 worth of pork chops — my husband won't be home for dinner."

"You ought to look at my naps as an economy measure. After all, if I weren't sleeping I might be eating."

"That will be nice to protect your eyes from the sun.
Now where's the top to the bikini?"

"Are you trying to bend over enough to TOUCH your
toes or just to see them?"

"How about an extra dollar . . . after all, it is for
your birthday present."

"You go ahead. I want to get tan, not blue!"

"Motivate me — remind me of that ever-growing stack of unpaid bills on the desk."

"And now after 19 years of marriage I'm still trying to be endowed with some of his worldly goods . . ."

"I have a feeling that we have burglars — why don't
you go downstairs and scare the
life out of them?"

"You know, I'm thinking of going into the grass hula
skirt business."

"You mean you've let a little tiny dog do what neither sleet nor snow nor gloom of night could do?"

"Free sample from a wake-up service."

"NOW you come up with sparkling retorts like 'You can be replaced by a meter maid.'"

"Don't worry about your husband finding out, lady — I'm not even sure I want to tell my mechanic!"

"Aren't you Internal Revenue people starting your reminders a little earlier this year?"

"To prove something to my husband, how about giving me a ticket for being seen in public in this last year's dress?"

"Got my Christmas gift from the boss."

"I call it 'souffle of leftover creamed leftover croquettes of Christmas turkey.'"

"So that's what the beard has been hiding all these years!"

"If you want me to carry something, hand me your wallet."

"This recipe was given to me by Mrs. Feeney . . .
now that Mr. Feeney has passed on she has no
further use for it."

"I see the TV industry is heavily into ecology . . .
they're recycling all the old series."

"You didn't get a balloon! How come? Did you bite the dentist?"

"Remember, it's five per cent off my price if your husband comes home while I'm working and you send him back out on an errand of some kind."

"I see all your meats have gone up in price except the frog legs. I thought they would be the first to jump."

"One guess who's salami and limburger cheese sandwich was voted by his office co-workers as 'the sandwich they'd like least to be stranded in an elevator with'!"

"Will the defendant please rise!"

"Well, we'll soon know whether toothpaste takes off whiskers as good as shaving cream."

"What's your down payment on a soup bone for my dog?"

"The doctor said 'slow down' — not come to a FULL STOP!"

"My talking to plants is no sillier than your talking back to the TV set."

"Another crushed alarm clock. That guy in there really loves his sleep."

"Suppose we observe our 75th anniversary now before we're too old to enjoy it?"

"You know, I think our car is beginning to get old
. . . have you noticed those new wrinkles
in the front fender?"

"If we aren't going anywhere this summer, we should
at least have some picture postcards
made of the house."

"I realize I'm a little late, but wouldn't you prefer that
to my being your LATE husband?"

"Only three-quarters of me belongs to you. Fifty of these pounds weren't there when we got married."

"Energy crisis is nothing new to him! He started it 20 years ago."

"I can remember when you used to say those kinds of nice things to me."

"Better write those words down. They're a natural to start stalled engines and fix leaky pipes."

"Need some quick-energy fuel to strengthen my re-
solve not to eat."

"My, what a green thumb you've suddenly
developed!"

"Quick, throw a coat over that bumper and look helpless!"

"You're all shaved and dressed and you've had breakfast. Okay, now here's the bad news — it's time to wake up and go to work."

"There'd better be something in my secret compartment, or we're in trouble."

"Keep a sharp alert for holdups until I get through depositing this seven dollars."

"May I have someone carry them to my car? All our
employees are fully bonded."

"Only a sadist would deliver a postcard from Florida
on a day like this."

"There's an armored truck outside. Are you expecting another delivery of hot dogs?"

"I'm not surprised that your tomato juice tasted odd. It's made from oranges."

"Shall we watch GOOD triumph in a play, or EVIL triumph in a newscast?"

"The boss told me I'd find a little something extra in my paycheck. Turns out it's a deduction for a new insurance plan."

"According to my pocket calculator, I paid $20 too much for my pocket calculator!"

"Hey, look, dear! It would be perfect for wrist wrestling."

"I'm trying to get up the nerve to wake him and tell
him that he got up on a Saturday morning
by mistake."

"Why don't you wear one of those instead of bundling
yourself up?"

"The boss wasn't REALLY coming for dinner. I just
was in the mood for a good meal."

"I tried to remember the financial news. As far as I
can figure it, Dow went up and Jones
went down."

"We now face only one shortage — money."

"I have the toughest Christmas shopping problem of
all . . . what to get the man who hates everything."

"What did you put in Mother's tea? She went to bed with her shoes on!"

"Why don't you make a little game of it and try to catch them before they hit the ground?"

"I'll certainly be glad when fall comes and you get back into civilian clothes."

"I wish you'd hang that hammock higher up where the leaves will hide you."

"Just pretend I'm your wife when you select those chops."

"Next summer I'm going to the mountains to get away from it all. 'It all' is going to the beach."

"I would have thought more of the speaker if he hadn't been wearing those alligator shoes."

"I sometimes wonder who St. Valentine was . . . most likely he was a candy merchant."

"You go ahead and have your 'happy hour' . . . I've had mine!"

"Does our insurance cover burned chicken?"

"Stanley rests only on those days of the week that end in 'y.' "

"That's a really brave police force we have. Two six-foot officers broke down and cried just watching me park."

"Wow! The trash man will have difficulty hauling that away!"

"It's just Mother's sense of humor. Actually, she's had your name memorized for almost six months now."

"He has an appetite like a hummingbird — eats twice his own weight daily."

"It only hurts when I flinch on seeing your bill."

"None of the OTHER husbands were whimpering."

"Say ... I didn't know you used to play country music!"

"And this ring Stanley gave me was a real heirloom,
handed down from gum-ball machine to
gum-ball machine."

"I've heard of green-keepers, but you're a green-
TAKER!"

"You'll find a water hazard in the kitchen — a sinkful of dishes awaits you."

"It is NOT a beautiful morning. Only the days beginning with an 'S' have beautiful mornings."

"Today I'm counting blessings instead of calories."

"What a day — I'll bet the snowman has put on fifty
pounds since I left this morning!"

"Don't go near him. If he sinks you might be pulled
under by the suction."

"I had some good news in the mail this morning, Stanley. All these bills were delivered by mistake
and belong to you."

"I'm off shopping this morning, so I'm charging you $5 for each cup of coffee, eggs are $3.50, and toast is $2 a slice. The jelly's on the house."

"That's not bad if you deduct five pounds for my clothing."

"Stop that HEAVY breathing on the scale!"

"Go get 'em tiger! . . . on second thought, try to stay even, pussy cat!"

"Don't growl at me! I didn't INVENT Monday morning. I just announce it."

"Are you doing anything besides listening to your arteries harden?"

"No dessert for me, thanks. I want to leave some room for the bicarbonate."

GOURMET FOODS

"I wish you were as brave about exotic and gourmet food at mealtime as you are at shopping time."